Supporting the

Highly Sensitive Child

Making Sense of Meltdowns

James Williams
and
Lucy Skye

A CIP catalogue record for this book is available from the British Library.

ISBN: 978-15427230-1-5

Book formatting by www.ebooksbydesign.co

Contents

Foreword by Lisa Nel, Children's Therapist MBACP (Accred)

Compassionate, guilt-reducing, informative and well-illustrated, this concise guide offers insight and practical support for any parent or professional ever faced with a child in 'meltdown' i.e. most parents and children's professionals!

Though written with specific reference to the highly sensitive child, as I read, many of the vulnerable children and young people with whom I've worked as a therapist kept popping into mind. While the reason a highly sensitive child is likely to reach meltdown quicker and more frequently than most children is due to their higher base level of anxiety and sensitivities, safely supporting meltdowns can challenge us all at some time. Feeling discomfort about change or future uncertainty and being easily 'triggered', are true of anyone with low emotional resilience, making this a fantastic and widely applicable resource. It is also notably of specific use for anyone who parents, teaches or supports a child on the autistic spectrum.

When a child experiences strong, uncontainable emotion, our responsibility as parents or professionals is to recognise and be a safe 'container' for their feelings. This both helps the child deal with the current moment as well as to gradually learn how to independently regulate, and understand the purpose of, feelings. As James and Lucy highlight, this doesn't mean having to always drop everything to 'be there' immediately, but being specific about when we can. Keeping our word is a reminder of how trust is a vital cornerstone of all relationships.

Safely supporting meltdowns takes its toll on us too and a key strength to this guide is the emphasis and ideas on compassionate self-care.

A good thing should always be shared! I hope that you will find this wonderful little book as helpful as I have and will pass it on to other parents and colleagues alike.

Lisa Nel
Children's therapist and founder of I'm OK, You're OK Social Enterprise
(www.imokyoureok.co.uk)

Introduction

Welcome to this short guide to making sense of meltdowns for the highly sensitive child. This book will give you a brief overview of meltdowns, how and why they occur, and how you can support them. This will help you to better understand yourself and highly sensitive children.

In each chapter you will find story scenarios (written in italics). These are based on our and others experiences, and you may be able to relate to some or many of them.

Parts of this book may feel hard to read at times. Don't be critical of yourself if you need to go through and process it over several sittings; meltdowns can be an emotive subject.

If you want more information about understanding highly sensitive children in general, you might want to start by reading the first book in this series, *Understanding the Highly Sensitive Child*.

A little about us

James:

I am privileged to be the primary carer for my two daughters and have been for over ten years. I feel passionately about the role of being a parent and truly believe it's the best job in the world. I am also acutely aware of how incredibly difficult and challenging it can be at times.

High sensitivity has a massive impact on my family's life, and coming to understand it has transformed our lives – for the better. Before we understood high sensitivity we were bumbling about in the dark; now we're in the light. I wish the entire world knew all about high sensitivity. What a wonderful world it would be if highly sensitive children and people were understood, accepted and truly valued for who they are.

All I can do is keep spreading the word, and hope that eventually everyone connected with children – teachers, health and medical professionals, care workers, parents etc. – recognise without judgement, value and nurture highly sensitive children.

During my Daddy years I have developed mindfulness practices through art, meditation and as a way of being. More recently I have started to train to be an Integrative Counsellor.

Lucy:

I have spent fifteen years supporting and working with children and families with different disabilities and needs. For the last six I have worked for a national autism charity and am hugely enthusiastic about improving awareness of hidden needs such as anxiety, sensory sensitivities and social communication, and supporting good mental health. I try to raise understanding of the impact of these needs on the wider family, particularly on siblings.

I am the author of a fiction book for children, *The Adventure of Maisie Voyager*. This won the Gold Medal at the Moonbeam Book Awards in 2012, and features a quirky protagonist with a range of high sensitivities, none of which stop her from getting fully involved in an exciting mystery. In most of my spare time I can be found either writing or running. Rarely both at once though.

I strongly identify as a highly sensitive person. Having this understanding has enabled me to improve my relationships and interactions with the world. This insight is continually growing and I believe that it is a path of life-long learning, and one I am happy to be on! Like James, I have recently started to train to be an Integrative Counsellor and look forward to embedding this into my life and work. .

Chapter 1: Meltdowns and highly sensitive children

Can you remind me what being highly sensitive means?

A highly sensitive child has a very sensitive nervous system, which can lead to:

1. Keen awareness – noticing many tiny details and subtleties in their environment

2. Intense experiencing – feeling emotions and sensations very deeply and strongly

3. Overload – being overwhelmed by the intensity of feelings and awareness

Overload may lead children to withdraw into themselves, to run away, or to react with frustration, fear or sadness. This point of overload is what we call a meltdown.

What is a meltdown?

Imagine a pot of metal shavings heating up in a forge. Each individual curl of iron gradually loses its shape and colour, eventually becoming an oozing blob of liquid.

Everything that was once solid has now lost its form and cannot hold its own shape any more.

Imagine a child bombarded: by requirements and requests from others, by sensory overload, by their own expectations. Every part of their brain is furiously firing away, trying to keep up with the demands. And then there is suddenly one more 'ask' of them, and this becomes the catalyst. All of their thoughts and feelings conflate; they are completely overwhelmed by these emotions that then burst out as fear or rage or sadness or frustration.

This is how a highly sensitive child experiences a meltdown.

What does a meltdown look like?

There is no clear answer to this – every child is an individual and will respond to situations differently depending on their level of distress or discomfort. You might recognise some of the following behaviours in your child, but will probably also be able to add several more to the list:

- Shouting
- Crying
- Withdrawing from activities
- Not speaking
- Using aggressive language
- Ignoring demands – not cooperating
- Kicking/hitting/biting – self or others
- Breaking or throwing things
- Running away
- Refusing to eat
- Hiding
- Absolute negativity

Meltdowns are not tantrums. A child having a meltdown is not consciously deciding to express their emotions in such a raw state in order to get their own way. They are not choosing to behave like this for their own gain. They are overloaded, and cannot contain their feelings any more.

Can you predict a meltdown?

We will look at the reasons for meltdowns occurring in the next chapter, but sometimes meltdowns can appear to come from nowhere.

An easy way to understand this is to think about an iceberg. The tip of the iceberg on the surface of the sea is the behaviour that you can see displayed by your child. But the iceberg actually stretches deep down into the water. This unseen volume represents all of the possible reasons for your child's behaviour occurring. You need to look below the surface to understand what might be hidden there.

Mum is keeping an eye on nine year old twins Oscar and Sam while they are playing Monopoly. The boys are talking and laughing quietly. Towards the end of the game Oscar gets a card that tells him to pay a fine. He suddenly throws the board across the room and stamps on the pieces. When Sam gets in his way, he pushes him over. Oscar shouts, 'It's not fair!' while running around and kicking the furniture in the room. Mum immediately tells Oscar that he needs to apologise and that he should know better. Oscar curls up on the sofa sobbing and will not talk to anyone.

Oscar is certainly old enough to 'know better' and to realise that he cannot always win. His behaviour comes across like a toddler's tantrum. But was he reacting to the 'bad' card or was there something else that was really happening for Oscar? What made him respond in this way?

Oscar is playing Monopoly with Sam, which is one of his favourite games, but lots of things are distracting. The next door neighbour is mowing the lawn and making a really irritating buzzing sound that makes Oscar's ears hurt. Oscar can't stop thinking about the maths test he did yesterday at school. They will get the results next week which seems a long time to wait. He wants to have done okay, but he just doesn't know. Before he and Sam started playing the game, Mum asked him to help make lunch later. Oscar doesn't know what he will need to do to help, or when 'later' is. Mum might take him away from the game at any point and he doesn't want to finish playing so he's worried about having to stop. Then Oscar gets a card that asks him to pay money. He's already had to do this twice and Sam hasn't had to at all. Why does Oscar always get the bad cards?

You cannot see any of these thoughts going on inside Oscar's head, but they are there. And picking the 'bad' card is not the reason for the meltdown, it is the final straw that has led to it occurring.

What can I do to help?

It is possible to start to recognise the build up to meltdowns, to try and prevent them before they occur, and understand the reasons why they might happen. You can also explore ideas as to how you can enable yourself to support your child, so that you can both have a better understanding of how to manage situations. This will help you to look after each other if a meltdown does occur.

High sensitivity in itself does not mean meltdowns are inevitable and there are ways you can prevent them. However there is no perfect fool-proof strategy, and it is important to be compassionate towards yourself, and your child, if they do occur. We will look more at all of this as we go through the book.

Chapter 2: Reasons for meltdowns

There are a wide range of reasons why meltdowns occur, and it can easily be a combination of several at any one time.

Emotional awareness

Emotions are complicated and tricky. We have basic words to describe them (such as happy, sad, and angry), but the physical feelings they create inside us, and the thoughts that often run alongside, make them much harder to truly understand.

How do we understand our emotions?

All of us have our own level of emotional literacy, which essentially means how well we understand our own emotions and how we express them. This understanding starts in early childhood and continues throughout our lives as we observe other people, read and learn about the world, and gain more comprehension about our own self. Emotional literacy is important because it helps us to recognise and respond appropriately to our emotions, enabling us take care of ourselves and to get our needs met.

Emotional literacy is not related to academic ability or age as there are many reasons why our understanding about our feelings can be compromised. Some of these include growing up in an environment where feelings are not discussed or expressed, or finding it difficult to recognise feelings in other people.

How might this affect my highly sensitive child?

Being highly sensitive is not related to having an introvert or an extrovert character. Many children may be very independent, giving the impression that they can manage situations well on their own, some precociously so. They may have learnt to mimic their peers to fit in while masking their true feelings, or they may be sensitive to other's feelings and do not want to 'burden' them. They may also have previously attempted to communicate their anxieties or stress, and had their feelings dismissed. This appearance of independence can be misleading. It is not always backed up with strong resilience, which means that children can consequently 'fall apart' or become overwhelmed very quickly. Because we presume that independent children have good emotional resilience, their meltdown may be dismissed as them being overtired or making a fuss for attention.

It is the final day of the Easter holidays before Esme goes back to school. This will be her last term in primary school. She has tests in a few weeks and the teachers keep talking about how important they are and how she must do her best. The exams mean that the normal school day routine will be different, but Esme doesn't know what will change. She has been feeling very worried about everything. At bedtime Dad comes to tell her that Gran will be taking her to school tomorrow instead of him. Esme feels panicky – she always talks to Dad in the car about her plans for the day, and now she won't be able to. She goes very quiet and stops getting changed into her pyjamas. Dad tells her to get a move on, but Esme refuses and will not talk or look at him. She thinks to herself that if she can stop going to bed, she can stop tomorrow coming and try and keep everything normal and calm. Dad gets more and more cross and tells her she needs to stop being silly, but Esme can't explain how she feels because everything is a muddle of anxiety and fear and stress and she doesn't know how to work out what to do.

Anxiety and stress

How do we manage stress?

When we feel angry or anxious, our body becomes physically alert. It gets us ready to run away or fight, 'fight or flight', a primitive response evolved for our own survival. Some of the physical signs showing our body is in this state include rapid breathing, tense muscles, higher heart rate, sweating, and increased adrenaline.

Your child may have a 'fight or flight' response when they are in a situation they find distressing. As a parent, you may have a similar response when confronted with your child having a meltdown. Being aware of your body's physical changes will indicate to you when you are in this situation. You can also help your child to be more aware of the physical changes in their own body to identify when they are experiencing heightened emotions. If you can identify when you are feeling angry or anxious, you can start to think about how to help ease these emotions. You can use this knowledge to react more rationally which will help you to maintain more control over your actions.

One of the most prevalent emotions for highly sensitive children is anxiety. Anxiety can be described as a general sense of worry or unease, and it can be a complex and overwhelming feeling. Anxiety may be driven by fear, although the fear itself may not always be able to be defined or specified. This can also become a problem in itself if you start to feel anxious about actually being anxious. When you have a thought that is attached to an unpleasant feeling, this feeling can then link into other thoughts that reinforce it. This risks you slipping into a cycle of negative and destructive thinking.

How anxious is my child?

We find it easier to understand anxiety resulting from obvious triggers such as taking an exam, meeting new people, starting a new school – anything where there seems to be a good reason for the emotion. However it is important to understand that highly sensitive children have a much greater base level of anxiety than children without high sensitivities. This means that it can take very little additional anxiety to push them into being extremely anxious. When anxiety is heightened to this extent it has a big impact on the way your child is able to process information and work out the best way to respond to situations.

Mum has asked Hannah to go to the shop with her. Now Hannah is screaming 'No! No! No!' and running up and down the stairs and around the house. When Mum get near she pushes her away, and thumps her. This hurts, and Mum shouts louder at Hannah, giving her warnings and finally telling her how she will be punished if she does not behave, which will involve limiting her time on the computer. Hannah gets more and more angry, kicking and slamming doors. She will not calm down.

*****

Hannah is reading her book and is told that she has to go to the shop as they've run out of milk. Hannah hates the shop as it is full of noises and smells and strange people. She doesn't usually go to the shop now, she goes on Saturday mornings with Dad. Today is not Saturday. And Hannah wants to finish her book. It's really exciting and if she doesn't finish now, she doesn't know when she will have time. Mum shouts up the stairs and tells her to get a move on, thinking that she hasn't heard the first time. The shout sounds like a cross voice and makes Hannah jump. Now she feels scared too, she doesn't know what's going on or what she's done wrong to make Mum drag her to a place she hates. Hannah panics.

Sensory experiences

Imagine if...

You ate some food that seemed like it was setting your tongue on fire – would you want to spit it out?

Someone patted your arm and it felt like they had just hit you with a hammer blow – would you recoil with pain or lash out?

Raindrops drumming on the roof sounded like bullets being fired next to your ears – would you try to block the noise?

Sensory sensitivities can lead to very positive, empowering experiences, however they can also cause a lot of discomfort creating difficulties focusing and interacting.

How sensitive is my child?

Highly sensitive children will feel things very intensely. Imagine that we all have an inner dial that regulates our sensitivity levels on a scale of 0-10. In general, our base level of sensitivity is a low 1-2. Highly sensitive children will have a base level of sensitivity several points above this, say 4-5 on the scale. When we are more stressed, anxious or in a situation that we find specifically challenging, our sensitivity level will rise. This means that highly sensitive children can become extremely overloaded by their sensitivities much more quickly as their base level is already so much higher.

This is similar to the levels of anxiety described earlier.

How do we use our senses?

We use our senses all of the time, and in any given situation have to learn to prioritise what are the most important ones to process information from.

Think about when you need to cross a busy road. You may experience the following sensations:

- Watching cars drive up and down the road
- Hearing the drone of car engines and beeps of car horns
- Smelling exhaust fumes
- Feeling the breeze as cars go quickly past
- Finding yourself dizzy and disorientated with cars speeding in multiple directions
- Holding your body tense and immediately ready to cross the road when there is space to do so

Being able to prioritise your senses means that you identify key information you need to help achieve your task successfully. Many highly sensitive children are so bombarded by the amount of sensory information they receive it is hard for them to filter what they need to focus on first. This can make it difficult to achieve tasks successfully and safely. It can also create a sensory overload.

> *Mum has taken the family out to a pizza restaurant for an end-of-term treat. Oscar is very excited and has been asking about it all week. Once they get to the restaurant he bounces around on his seat and orders his meal. Gradually more people arrive and it gets busier and noisier. Oscar quietens and sits still before sliding off his chair and crouching under the table. He won't talk or come out. Mum recognises that he is finding his surroundings hard to manage, and his earlier excitement has overwhelmed him to exhaustion. She lets him sit by her feet and play with her shoelaces as she talks to his*

brother Sam. When the pizza arrives, Mum asks if he will sit at the table but he does not respond. So she cuts some up and hands it to him. Oscar eats some food under the table, then crawls back up to his chair and finishes his meal quietly. Mum keeps talking to Sam and Oscar occasionally makes a comment, but Mum does not mention his change in position and avoids any focus of attention on him. There is no pressure at any point for him to get up and sit at the table, eat 'normally' or be part of the conversation. When they leave, Oscar says that he has enjoyed it and would like to go again, but maybe at a time when it will be a bit quieter.

What is sensory overload?

Sensory overload is when you are overwhelmed by the sensations you feel. When highly sensitive children experience overload, this is likely to lead to them having a meltdown. Children rarely have much control over their own environment and other people often make decisions for them. Even if your child is able to recognise the sensory experiences they find more difficult to tolerate, they may not be in a position to make them more tolerable. Also, your child may have a good understanding of their own senses but still have very strong reactions, which may lead to a meltdown because they are so physically affected by their sensory experiences.

This meltdown may mean they try to run away from the situation or shut down (literally shutting their eyes, blocking their ears or curling into a ball) to remove some of the discomfort that they are experiencing.

Mum asks Asha to lay the table for dinner. He gets the cutlery from the drawer and goes to set it out. Mum is clattering pans in the kitchen and he can smell onions frying in the pan. Asha hates onions. The smell makes him imagine the slippery texture in his mouth and he feels sick. His little sister is skipping around the table waiting for her food, getting in his way and making him bump into things. Now he can't remember which way round the knives and forks need to go as his head is so crowded with smells and noises and movement that there is no room for anything else. He looks at the cutlery in his hands and his face is distorted in the metal, the bright shiny surface hurts his eyes. Asha runs upstairs and hides under his duvet. The world is quiet, dark and peaceful there.

Communication

Our ability to communicate our feelings is key to our own self-acknowledgement and release, as well as assisting other people's understanding of our emotions.

What if it is difficult to communicate?

By their nature, highly sensitive children have strong emotional experiences, but that does not mean that they have a good recognition of their own emotions. They may not always have the words to understand what is going on, or they may not know how to put what they are feeling into words.

In some cases, children try to communicate their feelings, but this communication is not acknowledged. This may be because other people are too busy or distracted, or don't think it is important. The inability to communicate clearly, or communication that is misunderstood can be incredibly frustrating.

> *Oscar has been left out of a game by his friends. They are all laughing and having fun and he is on his own. As he watches them his tummy starts hurting and the pain just gets bigger. Oscar starts crying but when a teacher asks him what is wrong, all he can say is 'It hurts'.*

Oscar has not been able to link the physical pain to his feeling of sadness.

If children are able to communicate their feelings, they need to know how and when it is okay for them to express these. Bottled-up emotions can only stay contained for so long, and an overwhelming build up can lead to a meltdown.

Chapter 3: Your response to meltdowns

Children who are highly sensitive often worry excessively about little comments and actions others make. They may also feel unable to express their true feelings for fear of response, or because they do not feel that they are in an environment that is secure. This can lead to a bottling up of emotions, where your child tries to contain all of their thoughts and feelings until they are somewhere safe, which is often when they are at home.

Esme has been told that she can speak to her class teacher at lunchtimes if she is feeling upset or angry about anything. That morning, some girls in her class have been teasing her and calling her names. Esme ignores them but feels upset and cross inside. When she goes to talk to her teacher, her teacher tells her she doesn't have time as she has to attend a meeting. Esme feels lonely and anxious. Her worries build up all afternoon and as soon as she gets home she bursts into tears and shouts and screams at Mum and Dad and is unable to calm down.

Why do I need to think about my own response to meltdowns?

How has your child been responded to in the past when they've expressed their emotions?

They might have experienced some, or all of these:

- Given a cuddle
- Told off
- Told they are 'being silly'
- Not listened to (because other people are too busy)
- Sent to their room
- Emotions recognised, and supported and talked through
- Told to be quiet
- Shouted at

- Ignored
- Sent to another family member for them to deal with

What responses do you think you usually give?

How can I make sure I'm giving my child the response they need?

Unfortunately, what constitutes a 'good' time for a chat may not be when your child actually needs to talk. They're driven by their emotions and thoughts that cannot necessarily wait comfortably just because you're serving up dinner, going out the door to work, or they're in the middle of their maths homework. It can be easy for us to fool ourselves that we are listening while we're actually continuing to focus on other tasks. Think about how you can stop what you are doing when your child is talking. Really listen to what they are saying and take the opportunity to engage, to nurture this communication. The more you engage with your child to understand their emotions and reactions, the better able you will be to try to gauge the importance of what they want to say.

The thing is important to them if it is going to dominate their thoughts, if it is going to be impossible for them to move on until they are able to express themselves, if it is going to make them so anxious that holding it in may lead to a meltdown. Sometimes it might be important enough for you to have to be late for work or to postpone dinner but at other times, you might be able to delay the talk.

If you do delay the conversation, discuss with your child about making another time such as saying:

'We don't have enough time now to talk through everything because I have to go to work for a meeting about my project, but how about we go to the park when I pick you up after school and you can talk to me then? We will have lots more time if we do that and I can listen to you properly.'

Make sure that they know a definite point when they can talk so that there is an 'end' to how long they have to hold onto their thoughts for. You need to make sure that you follow this through, so they can learn to trust you and what you are saying. If you don't, then their trust will be dented – you can't expect your child to be trusting and honest with you if you aren't with them. If they know that you will give them time, that you mean what you say, then your relationship will be stronger.

Chapter 4: Discovering feelings

Recognising and communicating emotions

Some children find it very difficult to identify the emotions they are feeling and put them into words. Particularly when children are in a state of high anxiety they have a much more limited ability to think coherently and describe their situation in detail.

What if my child finds it hard to put their feelings into words?

It may be easier for your child to relate colours to emotions, or different visual images (such as a storm cloud for anger, and sunshine for happiness). Pointing to pictures, giving you a coloured card, or drawing an image, may be easier for them than saying the name of a feeling out loud.

Esme has created her own colour chart which relates a different colour to each feeling (yellow is anxiety, red is frustration, black is anger, purple is happy). She will either point to a colour or use her colouring pens to scribble how she feels.

What can help my child to understand their emotions?

Pictures of facial expressions may help your child to better identify and put a name to different emotions. You can use images of famous people, photos of family members, pictures of their favourite cartoon or TV characters, or drawings you or they have done. Talk to them about times when you observe they are happy, sad or angry and ask them how they physically feel inside their body. What are they thinking? How does their tummy feel? Do their limbs seem heavy, twitchy and agitated, bouncy or out of control? They may be able to use these physical triggers as a way of helping them to identify when they are experiencing certain feelings.

Asha loves reading comic books and drawing his own stories. When he needs to explain how he is feeling he will draw faces on cartoon characters and use them to describe what has triggered his emotions.

Hannah recognises that she bites her nails when she is becoming extremely stressed. She has asked her friends and family to tell her if they notice her doing it. When they do, she takes a moment by herself to try and work backwards to see what has been the trigger for her feelings. Then she can ask her friends and family to help with whatever is specifically worrying her.

An emotion chart can be a useful tool to help you and your child put together a plan to support their feelings, both positive and negative. You can cover as many emotions as you want. Your child might want to write it with you or create their own. It is important that they are involved as much as they feel able. This is much more likely to make it helpful and successful for you both, providing you with more insight to your child, and giving them ownership of the tool.

Oscar's Feelings Chart

When I feel...	I do this:	I can communicate this feeling to mum and dad by:	I can do this to make myself feel better:
Sad	Hide behind my bed	Telling them I need to hide somewhere	Go to my bedroom, shut the curtains and look at my glow stars
Cross	Tear things up	Ask for some paper I can rip	Rip the paper and stand on my bed and scatter it onto the floor
Happy	Skip on the spot and talk very quickly	Telling them what I am happy about	-
Scared	Stop talking and pull my hair	Draw a picture of what I am scared of	Wrap myself in a blanket or have a hug
Excited	Ask lots and lots of questions	Writing down what I am excited about	-
Anxious	Jump around like the butterflies in my tummy	Get their attention and flutter my fingers like butterflies	Have my fingers held tight until I can write down what I am anxious about
Sleepy	Rub my fingers together and cuddle a cushion or toy	Giving them the cushion so they know I want to go to bed	

Chapter 5: Adjusting and noticing

While you seek guidance and tips for managing meltdowns, what you really want to do is to try and prevent them from occurring in the first place. This involves a little detective work and a lot of patience...

You will also need to equip yourself for the task. You will need to think about your own emotional response to your child's meltdown. How do you engage with them before, during and after the meltdown occurs? What does the experience leave you feeling like? How do you take care of yourself throughout this process?

You want to be strong for your child but this does not mean you should block out your own emotions, quite the opposite. While you may have to delay or defer your emotional response to a meltdown, you absolutely need to give your emotions the space and acknowledgement required in order to be able to give your child what they need.

What's the best way of understanding the triggers and recognising my response?

You might find it useful to keep a notebook with you and record daily events and any meltdowns that occur. While it is useful to look at what happened during the meltdown itself, you are only going to find the triggers for the meltdown by identifying preceding events. It is important to realise that these triggers may not be isolated to immediately before the meltdown, and there could be a gradual build-up over several hours, days or even weeks.

Each day write down:

- How your child seems in general (happy, relaxed, anxious etc.)
- Key activities, situations and environments that cause them visible anxiety or stress
- How you respond to these moments of anxiety or stress
- How you feel that day in general
- How you feel after your child's anxious or stressed moments

Try and do this for a few weeks to build up a good picture of how things go day to day. Then give yourself some time to go through the notes and see if there are any common patterns occurring.

Having this insight will start to give you a clearer picture of the parts of life that you and your child find more difficult. Recognising these means you can start to put support strategies in place.

Asha's Week

Mum has been keeping a diary for a few weeks. Going through her entries, she can start to see where points of anxiety for Asha are, and where he hasn't always been supported (for whatever reason).

Monday

Asha's general mood: *He got things ready for school last night so was well prepared, he seemed happy all day.*

Anxiety/stress situations: *Wanted to finish game on computer before he went to bed.*

My response: *Gave him two warnings and he came off without grumbling.*

How I felt after any situations: *Pretty chuffed – I stuck to my decision about the computer and things remained calm. I felt in control!*

My general mood: *Positive – good day at work and kids were well behaved.*

Tuesday

Asha's general mood: *Out of sorts and grumpy. Came home very upset.*

Anxiety/stress situations: *Worried about his football match at school. His team lost the match.*

My response: *Didn't have time to talk – late for work. Left him on computer to wind down.*

How I felt after any situations: *Didn't have any patience and just wished he could behave. Guilty for relying on technology!*

My general mood: *Bit stressed as worried about Asha's day as well as chairing an important meeting.*

Wednesday

Asha's general mood: *Reasonable until a big argument tonight. Calm by bedtime.*

Anxiety/stress situations: *Kids were talking about football at tea and Asha threw his plate across the room.*

My response: *I shouted, he yelled back and followed me around arguing for ages before finally going to his room.*

How I felt after any situations: *Felt as though I had no control and couldn't get through to Asha. Situation seemed to end on its own but not sure how.*

My general mood: *Exhausted as didn't sleep well last night because I missed a deadline at work. Argument was last straw.*

Thursday

Asha's general mood: *Refused to get out of bed, talk, or look at me first thing this morning. Quiet and subdued tonight.*

Anxiety/stress situations: *No clear issues! Seemed calm the night before and nothing going on at school or home.*

My response: *Shouted, tried to bargain, but no response. Finally just sat in room with him before he eventually started to talk.*

How I felt after any situations: *When he started talking I knew things would improve and it was a breakthrough. We both calmed down and he let me take him to school.*

My general mood: *Very tired and teary but finally more relaxed by end of day. Realised that sometimes Asha needs to come to me in his own time and I can't force a solution.*

Friday

Asha's general mood: *Happy and chilled out Asha!*

Anxiety/stress situations: *None - looking forward to a weekend at home.*

My response: *Watched a film together and had an evening laughing and joking.*

How I felt after any situations: *Hopeful, I feel like I have a bit of a plan for future situations.*

My general mood: *It's been a long week but a good end.*

What sort of environments will be most supportive?

A 'low-arousal' environment is a space that places minimal stress upon your child, where they can feel calm and relaxed. This will be different for every child, depending on the things they find challenging or stressful. We all require this kind of environment at times in order to recharge our energy levels, give ourselves time to process information, or simply get away from demands on us. If we don't have access to this we can find it hard to keep functioning productively, becoming emotionally drained and exhausted.

You want to try to have access to the sort of low arousal environment that you need. Think about the moments when you find space, peace or relaxation. This could be a drink in a pub with friends, a relaxing bath, sitting down listening to music, or a walk in the countryside. What is it that you need, to be at your best? You will be busy with many priorities, however taking even ten minutes of time for yourself as regularly as you can, will be of benefit to all of your life and relationships.

It is rarely possible to ensure that we are in the 'best' environment all of the time. The world around us can be quite inflexible to individual needs! However, if you know that you are going to places that you or your child find more stressful, try and build in time in a more supportive environment before and afterwards. This 'down time' will help to recharge resilience levels.

What if I'm having a day when I'm not feeling good?

Your child may be more highly sensitive to your emotions as well as their own. Consider how well you currently communicate your emotions to your child and whether you share reasons for your feelings. Imagine a day at work where nothing goes to plan – your computer crashes, clients are unresponsive, a deadline has been brought forwards, traffic is bad. When you get home you are tired, snappy and short tempered because of the difficulties in your day. Your child is aware of your frustration and angry feelings because of your outward behaviours, but do they know the cause? They may believe that they are the source if they have no other explanation, which can lead to their own challenging feelings such as confusion, guilt and anxiety, resulting in a meltdown.

You do not need to relay every detail of what is causing your emotions, but an honest and simple explanation is easily understood: 'I am sorry if I'm not very patient tonight but I've had a hard day at work, I'm not cross with you even if it sounds like I am.' This clarity will help your child to avoid blaming themselves as being the cause of your feelings and allow them to see your emotions in context.

How do I stop feeling guilty if I am not putting my child first all the time?

Having an insight to your own needs may also make you acutely aware of your own vulnerabilities and this can feel very painful. Many of us are apt to focus on what we haven't done right, what we aren't able to do – anything we perceive as our personal 'failings'. In reality, the fact that you have this awareness is a huge strength. This 'noticing' is an asset, because by noticing and reflecting on your actions you can make more conscious choices about how to behave and respond. This may include being more compassionate to yourself if things don't always go to plan!

Making time to look after yourself will give you greater capacity to understand your child's needs, and strengthen the bond you share.

Dad spends all of his spare time reading about high sensitivity and adapting his home to be a less stressful environment so that he can better understand and support his son Oscar. He is so determined to be there for Oscar that he does not take any time for himself, or consider how difficult he is finding the demands of managing his roles at work and at home. He's so driven to be the best parent he can that he finds himself getting frustrated when the interventions he puts in place do not work. He is tired, but will not let himself relax in case he misses a chance to learn something new, or improve some part of Oscar's life. This tiredness is making him irritable and short-tempered with his family and he is finding it harder to be tolerant and patient in difficult situations. Every interaction with Oscar feels like a confrontation about how he is coping, even though he means it in a caring way.

Dad is unhappy with how he is managing the situation and he decides to take a day off work to have some space by himself. He goes fishing, something he hasn't done since Oscar was a baby. While he is sitting quietly by the river, he feels a sense of calm and relaxation that hasn't been with him for months. He considers how Oscar might enjoy coming fishing and being quiet with him too, without having to talk or feel pressured into behaving in a particular way.

Now, on one day a month, Dad goes fishing for a few hours on his own. He schedules this into the calendar so that Oscar knows he will not be home in advance. On another day in the month, he also takes Oscar out fishing with him, and they can both relax.

Dad feels he has more patience and is able to just focus on time with Oscar, without thinking about what he should be doing next.

Will doing all of these things stop my child from having a meltdown?

Meltdowns will occur, however much you try to understand the reasons why, put plans in place, or moderate your own actions. It may feel impossible but you can learn to live with meltdowns happening sometimes and be okay with this, as long as you have an outlet for your own emotions and avoid being too self-critical. Meltdowns are not a reflection of you doing too little, you simply cannot always predict every situation that your child will face. However understanding the reasons behind meltdowns will help to minimise their occurrence, and hopefully their impact, helping you and your child to be more empowered.

Chapter 6: When meltdowns occur – supporting your child

Meltdowns can be big or small, can take place in public or at home, can be filled with anger or sadness or fear. All are challenging for children and for others around them to manage.

Can I make a difference wherever meltdowns take place?

Your home is the environment you have the most control over, and consequently can feel the safest place to be. Is there a particular area where your child feels comfortable and protected? Talk to your child, or observe the places they seem most relaxed or seek out when they are stressed. This could be their bedroom, in the garden, or under blankets on the sofa. If you can encourage your child to move into this place (or quietly steer them in that direction) at the start of a meltdown, this will immediately give them the reassurance of being in a more secure surrounding.

If you are out when your child has a meltdown, this may feel more demanding as the surroundings are unfamiliar and there may be other people to contend with. Try to block out any distractions, focus on your child, what you know they are trying to communicate and what they need. Create a space that is as calm and sensitive as possible – move to a quiet area, sit down in a corner by a wall, or sit or stand in front of your child so that they feel more enclosed and less vulnerable.

Think about what particular activities your child finds relaxing or enjoys talking about. If you can see they are building up to having a meltdown, distracting them may divert their attention and reduce their anxieties. If your child has gone into a full meltdown, it is unlikely that they will have the space in their head to be able to fully engage and they may find the distraction attempt more stressful. Usually the only way of telling whether they are able to engage is to gently try, being sensitive to whether it is increasing their distress, which will help you to work out whether to persevere or not.

Hannah has huge anxieties about any medical procedures. She needs to have some routine injections, and knows why they are important, but every time she tries she ends up refusing to go into the doctor's surgery and Dad can't get her past the front door. He talks to her about what she is worried about. Hannah does not want to wait around lots of other people before she goes in. She also does not want to see the needle in her arm. They work out a plan together. Dad contacts the surgery in advance to tell them about her anxieties and request that they wait outside until the appointment time, when the nurse will come and get them. As they walk through, Dad stands in front and shields her from people walking in and out. Hannah keeps her head down and her headphones on with some favourite music. She goes straight to the clinic room and onto the bed, where she pulls the curtain around so that she cannot see the rest of the room. Then her music stops working. Hannah wants to leave and is getting very upset. Dad starts talking to her about her favourite bands and they try to remember the names of the songs she likes best. Hannah agrees to stay for the injection, and puts her arm through the gap in the curtain and hides her face, so she doesn't have to see it or interact with the nurse. After it is done, she spends a few minutes sitting quietly, before Dad walks her safely back to the car. Both of them are really pleased at how well she has managed to cope.

How can I make sure I can support everything that might be a problem?

It may be very tempting to try to overcompensate for any difficulties your child experiences, and to restrict their environment to try to make it 'absolutely right'. Yet this simply isn't possible – the world is incredibly diverse, and there will be many situations your child finds themselves in that are contradictory to their needs. While you want to create safe spaces, there also has to be a level of exposure even if this is very tough for your child to experience and for you to witness. If children can risk experiences, they can better understand their own limits and how to look after themselves, while in these environments and afterwards. When your child is very young, this may not be realistic. As they get older you will continue to be there to provide support and understanding but they can also start to build their resilience to cope in situations on their own.

Be brave and support your child to be brave too – they may surprise you! Don't always presume that your child will not be able to cope. Try to consider whether it is your anxieties that are shaping your decisions, rather than your child's.

Esme has a close group of three friends. One of them is having a birthday sleepover. Esme is very excited but very scared about staying away from home. She has planned to go to sleepovers before but always got too anxious and cancelled at the last minute. Mum is concerned that she will not manage it this time. This will be another dent to her confidence as she already worries that she is different to her friends.

Mum and Esme talk it through. Esme really wants to try, and gets frustrated when Mum warns her about how she might feel if she doesn't manage. They make a plan that Esme will go but Mum will pick her up at 9pm unless Esme calls to say she is staying over. That way she has a way out if she cannot manage and won't feel trapped.

Even though she is anxious on the day, Esme goes to the sleepover. She does go home at 9pm, because she decides she's had enough and wants the familiarity and quiet of her own bedroom. However she doesn't feel that she has failed because she stayed up late with her friends, and she was part of the group in a way that she could manage.

Mum is pleased that Esme set her own goals, and recognises what an achievement it was to stay out that late (something Mum didn't expect), even if she couldn't ultimately stay overnight.

How do I manage other people being around when my child has a meltdown?

During a meltdown, your child may want you or another familiar person near them to provide reassurance. Alternatively, some children may want to be left completely alone until they are in a calmer frame of mind. If your child prefers to be by themselves, remove as many other people from the environment as possible – ask siblings to go into another room, or move your child to a quiet place such as a corner of the park or the rear of a shop if you are out. It may be helpful for your child to shut their eyes, wear a hat or put headphones in to block any immediate sensory difficulties. If it is safe to, give your child the space they seek – observe from a distance, or situate yourself in the room next door. Make sure you let them know where you are, what you are doing, and that you will be checking on them so that they are clear about what is happening and how to reach you if they need.

Whether your child is tolerant of other people or oblivious to them while they are having a meltdown, you will want to minimise any impact that they can have on your child and yourself.

> *Esme did not sleep well and wakes up tired and out of sorts. She does not want to go to school but Dad gets her into the car without much difficulty. When Esme gets into the playground however, she starts crying and shaking and will not go near any of the other children. As her crying increases, the other children and parents start staring. Dad takes her round to the school reception. Usually no-one is allowed into the building until the bell rings, but the head teacher has said that Esme can use this area as a quiet place if she is finding the start of the day hard. There are no other people in the room, and Dad takes her to the furthest corner where he sits her down so she is facing the wall. Dad gives her a beanbag to throw at the wall and to squish in her hands. He waits by the front door so that he is still nearby, and she cannot run away. Esme takes all of her cross feelings out on the beanbag, and gradually stops crying. When she is sitting quietly, stroking the soft fabric of the bag, Dad goes back to her and she asks him for a hug. By the time the bell rings, Esme is calm enough to go into class, and takes the beanbag with her as reassurance.*

My other children find it hard when their sibling has a meltdown – how can I support them too?

If you have other children, you may have concerns about them experiencing their sibling's meltdowns. During the meltdown itself, make sure that they are safe and reassure them about what is happening. If you can, encourage them to distract themselves with something they enjoy, away from their sibling. After the meltdown, once your highly sensitive child is more settled, check with your other children how they are feeling and if they need to talk about anything. Encourage them to be as honest as possible and try to give them the time they need to be the centre of your focus. They may express feelings of fear or anxiety, or they may show anger towards their sibling, particularly if an activity has been interrupted. Provide reassurance, and gently explain why the meltdown might have occurred if you can.

It can be difficult to try and make sure you give all of your children enough time and space to feel that they are of equal priority. Some may develop a very responsible role, intuitive to their highly sensitive sibling's emotions. Being so aware of the overwhelming nature of their brother's or sister's feelings may make them believe that their emotions are less valid, or should be hidden, in order not to take up your time. They may talk to you a lot about activities and interests, but avoid the topic of their feelings. Consciously tell your children that they can come to you to express their feelings – however raw or wild – and that they are given space to freely express themselves (don't assume that they will automatically know this). Let them know that feelings are okay, and it is alright to show them safely. Their sibling's increased emotional needs doesn't mean that theirs are not valid too.

What can I do to manage my own emotions and reactions during a meltdown?

Perhaps the most challenging element of a meltdown is holding on to your emotions and focusing on your child, which is why we encourage so much self-care! Public meltdowns are likely to arise strong feelings for you, including those of shame and embarrassment, which can trigger our own 'fight or flight' response. Consequently, you may feel like you want to disengage with your child, avoid particular places where meltdowns have previously occurred, or not go out in public at all (which can be draining and restricting).

It is not at all easy to stop caring about what other people might think, but *you* know your child is your priority. Considering other people's observations or opinions too much may stop you from concentrating your thoughts towards easing your child's emotional distress and identifying the cause. The more you can focus on your child during their meltdown, the more likely you are to provide the best support and assistance to them, and yourself too.

The more you can be present with your child in general, the easier it will be to hold onto that positive connection during challenging moments. Remind yourself of the joy and closeness that you share with your child, and use them to try and bring your thoughts onto the person your child is, and not their behaviour. This is where you will find your strength in really difficult times.

You do not want to ignore your feelings completely, and keeping a journal or diary can be a good way of recording your emotional responses and allowing yourself time to recognise and reflect. It may be difficult to acknowledge some of the more painful emotions, particularly if these include feelings of guilt. Try to be honest without involving blame or shame, towards yourself or others. You may feel anger, but this does not mean you are an angry person – you are experiencing an emotional response to a situation, it does not define everything you are.

If a meltdown occurs, you may immediately consider everything that you think you haven't done 'correctly'. Some people try to take responsibility for everything, in order to feel more in control (after a situation that has felt very 'out of control'). This isn't helpful for you or for your child. However engaged and in-tune you are to your child's needs, remember everyone is fallible and situations are always changing. We are often quick to rush to judgement, but take time to recognise the positive actions and changes you have made, and are making. This will help you to manage situations more effectively and have belief in your strength and ability to continue to do this.

Mum takes Oscar to the big adventure park as a treat after school. There are lots of other children there running and screaming and Oscar finds it a bit overwhelming. He spends a long time waiting for his turn at the slide before another boy suddenly pushes in front.

Oscar starts throwing bits of wood at him and he pushes him back. Mum finds Oscar screaming, lying and kicking on the floor with some children pointing and laughing. Parents come over to pull their children away, muttering comments like 'If that was my child...', 'His mother should be ashamed...', 'They shouldn't allow children like that here.' One father asks her gently if he can be of any help, but Mum can't respond. All Mum wants to do is leave and get away.

Mum talks calmly to Oscar until he is less distressed and gets him safely home. Later that night, when Oscar is in bed, Mum is very upset. She feels like she doesn't ever want to go back to the park again, and that she doesn't want to go out with Oscar in case he becomes distressed and has a meltdown. Mum feels ashamed, as if she cannot cope, and doesn't know how to manage things for the best.

What Mum and Oscar experienced was horrible. The emotions Mum went through as a result, could have paralysed her relationship with Oscar and with other people, particularly if these meltdowns kept happening. They made her feel like she wanted to avoid contact with anyone, and avoid any situations that might trigger a meltdown for Oscar. But what is most important is that Mum recognised this.

Once Mum is able to express her distress, she is then also able to identify how she feels and to think a bit more clearly. She remembers the one parent who had offered to help her and Oscar. He had seen how distressed they both were and wanted to make it better. Mum knows that Oscar is her absolute priority, the one thing she loves more than anything in the world. She does not want the distraction of other people's negative opinions to stop her from trying to focus on him at a time when he most needs it, particularly when those opinions are not true of everyone's.

It would be very hard to honestly say that you do not ever care at all about other people's thoughts and reactions, but when your child is having a meltdown, the only thing you really wants to focus on is them. If you go out and a meltdown occurs, concentrate on trying to work out what is causing the distress and what you can do to ease it. This will block your mind (somewhat) from overhearing unnecessary comments, or observing any negative reactions. Ultimately the experience may still hurt, so it is very important to allow yourself time to express your emotions and seek reassurance or comfort later on once your child is calm and safe and you have been able to process events.

Some days I just don't feel able to do any of these things and I can't help my child. What do I do then?

With the best of intentions, these days will happen – remember that you are not alone and however bad you feel that you are not doing the 'right' thing for your child, it doesn't make you a bad person or a failure as a parent! Getting it 'wrong' is natural. We all do it, and it's also important to share that fact with your child when you can.

Keep your child as safe and secure as possible while they are having a meltdown. Give them time to calm down, and time for your emotions to feel more stable. When your child is calm and can listen to you, talk to them about what you think you did this time that wasn't helpful and also the reasons for why you did it. This can show your child you are trying your best, and are on their side, whilst also recognising that you are not perfect. It's a great way for them to see a demonstration that getting things wrong is okay and isn't reflective of who you are as a person or how hard you are trying.

Asha doesn't want to go into school. He refuses to get out the car and won't move from his seat. Mum is worried about a meeting at work, and she needs to get there on time. She tries to hurry Asha up, but he will not talk to her, and she ends up shouting at him. Other children and parents are walking past the car and start pointing and staring. Mum is embarrassed, which makes her shout at Asha even more, but it makes no difference to his behaviour.

Then Asha bursts into tears and tells her he has forgotten to do some homework. Mum feels guilty and tries to calm him down, but he gets more upset. She stops trying to talk to him and just sits with him until he is quieter.

Mum tells Asha she is sorry for shouting and that she is worried about getting into work because of her meeting. This means she wasn't able to be as patient as she would like and tries to be.

Asha stops crying. She asks him what would help him to go into school. He asks her to write a note to explain about the homework and once she has done this, he agrees to go in.

While it would have been ideal if Mum had been able to fully focus on Asha from the beginning, the fact she wasn't able to was very understandable. By being honest with him, they were both able to start communicating more clearly again.

Even getting things wrong can lead to strengthening of relationships – allow that positive outcome to be created for you and your child.

Chapter Seven: Caring for yourself, caring for your child

Parenting is probably the hardest occupation on the planet and rarely gets recognised as such.

What if I get things wrong?

You want to be a parent who is present and aware for your child. Sometimes this will feel wonderfully easy, and the pieces of the puzzle will fall straight into place. But sometimes this is going to be more difficult. If you don't know where to start, or you try something and it goes wrong, this doesn't mean that you have failed your child, or that you are a rubbish parent. It's part of the bumpy ride of parenting.

When things don't go to plan, there are two options – to feel guilty and berate yourself for not doing 'better', or to recognise that you did what you could at that time, and that was all that was possible. Guilt is incredibly self-destructive, and limits your thinking. Guilt makes you focus on yourself and your perceived shortcomings, rather than looking at what you can learn from an experience, about yourself and your child. Show some tenderness towards yourself, you are not a failure just because you had a bad day or showed impatience or intolerance; you are human.

How can I better engage with my emotions?

Our timetables and daily schedules channel us into being disengaged in order to function and just get through the day. Emotions can get in the way of this – they are confusing and overwhelming and distracting. They take time to understand and to support. We may need to consciously plug ourselves back in to our emotions when we get too detached. While this may add more complication to your general day, it is a healthier and more honest state in which to exist in. You will benefit from noticing the tiny things that touch your emotions positively: your child's smile when you truly listen to their words, their hand in yours as you walk along the road, the mealtime that passes peacefully without incident or argument...

Trying to avoid emotions may inadvertently lead to you experiencing increased feelings of guilt or frustration when you cannot respond to your child in the way, or with the time, that you want to. One of the most complicated and overwhelming feelings to manage is shame. Shame can be so polarising that we want to physically and emotionally disengage with other people, run or shut ourselves away, or erase moments from our past. Shame is ultimately self-destructive and does not help us to change for the future.

Having a child who is highly sensitive means that you may need to adjust some priorities at times. That hour you scheduled to hoover the house might need to be set aside to talk through your child's feelings about an incident at school. At the end of the day, there will still be crumbs and fluff on the floor, but you and your child will be strengthened by having the time and space to be heard.

There's more to our family than just me and my child...how can we all work together?

If you are parenting in a partnership, you are likely to both have differing levels of understanding about your child and the way they react and respond to situations (this is also the case with other family members and carers involved in your child's life). This is completely natural given our individuality and the unique emotional make-up we all have, but this difference can sometimes lead to conflict. One of you may completely 'get' your child and be able to intuitively pick up on the emotional cues that they display and respond to what they need. One of you may find it much harder to relate to any difficulties, or to recognise why your child becomes overwhelmed. You both have your child's best interests at heart, but may not be able to work at the same pace to achieve this. This can lead to arguments if you feel your partner is being too strict or negative towards your child, or if you feel frustrated because you desperately want to understand your child better but your partner seems to find it so much easier. Tiredness and the general demands of family life are additional pressures.

If you have a different approach to your partner, this can mean that you find yourselves at odds when your child is having a meltdown.

During a family evening meal at the dinner table. Hannah becomes quiet and starts sobbing because it is too noisy. Mum tells her that she can take her plate into the kitchen and sit and eat there quietly, but Dad intervenes, he wants a meal together and he tells Hannah's sisters to be quiet and stop chattering. They start to protest about how it isn't fair. Mum and Dad argue with each other, while Hannah gets more upset. Her sisters stop eating and get cross. Eventually, Dad gets up and goes to finish his meal in the other room. Everyone is left feeling very wretched.

You can see both sides here, each parent is trying to do the 'right' thing to support Hannah, but in the process of disagreeing no-one's needs are met, and everyone is left wanting. Each family member has a deficit of comfort and reassurance.

Making decisions together with your partner, forming a common approach, will give your child reassurance and will help to develop a stronger bond with your partner. This takes time, as you talk together, not just about your child's sensitivities, but also about your own emotions and understanding. Conversations about supporting your child can easily become solely focused on your child's needs, but actually the people caring for them have needs of their own. Supporting your needs, and those of your partner, reinforces your family unit. It means that you are stronger, better able to manage the meltdowns and other challenges, that your child can feel safe, whoever is caring for them.

So it's a bit of a balancing act?

Yes! You will always be seeking to find the balance between caring for your child, looking after yourself, and having time together with your partner and/or other children. While this balance may not always be perfect, try to keep in mind the importance of each element for an emotionally successful life.

Making it happen

Managing meltdowns takes time, it won't happen overnight and you will make plenty of mistakes along the way. Gradually build your capacity for compassion and understanding towards yourself and your child, and your knowledge and strength in understanding and managing meltdowns will only increase. You will feel more in control, and your child will have a strong source of support to help them thrive.

Believe in yourself, and believe in your child.

Keep up with our latest news, books and thinking here:

https://www.facebook.com/myhighlysensitivechild

https://twitter.com/FamilyFeelings

http://familyfeelings.today

Made in the USA
San Bernardino, CA
20 June 2018